SENTIMENTS

Michael Colavito

Order this book online at www.trafford.com
or email orders@trafford.com

Most Trafford titles are also available at major online book retailers.

Printed in the United States of America.

ISBN: 978-1-4907-3286-2 (sc)
ISBN: 978-1-4907-3285-5 (e)

Because of the dynamic nature of the Internet, any web addresses or links contained in
this book may have changed since publication and may no longer be valid. The views
expressed in this work are solely those of the author and do not necessarily reflect the
views of the publisher, and the publisher hereby disclaims any responsibility for them.

Any people depicted in stock imagery provided by Thinkstock are models,
and such images are being used for illustrative purposes only.
Certain stock imagery © Thinkstock.

Trafford rev. 03/31/2014

 www.trafford.com

North America & international
toll-free: 1 888 232 4444 (USA & Canada)
fax: 812 355 4082

TO MY FRIENDS IN PWP
WHO HAVE STAYED BY MY SIDE

AND

TO MY FRIENDS AT STATEN ISLAND UNIVERSITY
HOSPITAL WHO HAVE ENCOURAGED ME TO
"GO FOR IT"

THIS BOOK IS GRATEFULLY DEDICATED

CONTENTS

MY WRITING BOOK

All the beauty of life I see with my eyes

I put in my writing book

All the glory of Heaven I see in the skies

I put in my writing book.

All the happy, the sad, the good, and the bad
The loves I saw a long time before
The hopes and the dreams I search, always, for
The questions which live in my mind, evermore

I put in my writing book.

When I feel lonesome - Feeling so blue
When there's no place to go
When there's nothing to do
When I want to remember the good I once knew

I look in my writing book.

My writing book is a memory
Of the life I've lived in the past
Each page is a day of the life I knew
The days which never did last.

I'll write every day as I go on my way
So tomorrow I can see, then
The life I am living this very day
I will never live, ever again

Except -

In my writing book.

THE SANDS OF LOVE

Come with me to the empty beach
Walk with me in the sand
Let me pretend you're mine tonight
As we walk hand in hand

Help me find a starfish
Washed up by the sea
Let's sit and tease the edge of tide
And imagine you love me

Let's write our names within the sand
As though you were my love
Let's lie down on our backs awhile
And watch the moon above

Let's spend the night together
Only you and me
Pretending that we two are one
As the sand is to the sea

Then when it's time for us to leave
Some sand, please, give to me
To help me never to forget
Your beautiful memory

SOMEONE CARES

When life seems blue and all in vain
When in place of joy is found only pain
When the road you walk is wet with rain

There's always someone who cares.

When the mountain you climb has no top
When you lose your way and you want to stop
When the hope you carry seems to always drop

There's always someone who cares.

Turn your head and look around
Lift your eyes up off the ground
Set your sights and set them high
Look for the sunshine in the sky
The steps of life are there to climb
Take each step one at a time
And keep in mind as you climb the stairs

There's always someone - someone who cares.

If you don't believe what I say is true
Give me your hand, I care for you

MY KIND OF WOMAN

Did God make a woman for my eyes to see
A woman who likes the same things as me
I've searched and I've searched, traveled far and wide
For one to share my interests, to stay by my side.

No fast cars, no loud bars, these things are not for me
Firesides and kiddie rides are the things I like to see
A little home in the country with flowers, grass and trees
Children running all about scraping hearts and knees.

Cuddling by the fireside at the end of day
Speaking words of life and love while hearing music play
Sharing life together, just home and family
Enjoying all the beauty of nature there to see.

To live for one another the way I like to live
To make each other happy to always want to give
To do things as a family, what more can there be
Did God make such a woman like that *for me?*

MAY YOU NEVER WANT

May the beauty, the bright, the smile of the sun
Find home within you and come, never, undone
May the breeze which dances through branches of trees
Carry love, bear joy, for your life to seize.

May all the blessings, from God, we pray
Abide within you, day by day
May the wishes, the hopes, the dreams your mind seek
Be instilled in your life week after week.

May smiles and laughter possess, ever, your face
Happiness, month by month, may you ever embrace
May strength and faith conquer always your fear
And grow taller than mountains year after year.

May you never need your entire life through
May decade by decade life, to you, be true
May you always find love more than ever before
And rule your life score after score.

May you never see hardship
Despair or strife
May you never want
Throughout your life.

ASLEEP OR AWAKE

A little house on top of a hill
Surrounded by some trees
Plenty of grass and flowers
Swaying gently in the breeze

Many happy children running all around
Laughing, jumping, rolling, playing on the ground
Some chickens and some rabbits, a little puppy, too
Birds flying here and there in the sky so blue

A man and a woman
Standing hand in hand
Enjoying all these wonders they see
There on their very own land

The feeling of true love
Showing on their face
Thankful for the gifts they have
Given by God's good grace

A life like that to many a folk
Ridiculous may seem
But you just looked inside my mind
And saw my lifelong dream

THOUGH APART, TOGETHER

We're apart, far apart and perhaps, ever, will be
Yet, my darling, you share the same joys with me
Your eyes see the Moon and the Stars in the sky
I, too, behold these sights with each night gone by

The Sun gives you warmth as a lover's embrace
So to me glows the Sun amidst its Heavenly place
The air you breath I share with you love
The sprinkle of raindrops showers us both from above

The snows kiss you softly as they float smoothly down
As I feel their love in their flight to the ground
The Cloud you see rolling, joyfully, by
Is shared with you, darling by the sight of my eye

All the beauty, the wonders, of life there to see
I share with you though I know not whom you be
Yet someday I pray, if God's will be done
Together we will share Heaven's love two as one

THE MOST BEAUTIFUL GIFT TO ME

Nothing more beautiful
Will I ever see
Than this truly great gift
Given to me

Never through time
Will I ever say
I've been given more
Than I've received on this day

No bigger treasure
No thing of more worth
Will I ever receive
In my life on this earth

This one beautiful gift
Worthless, makes other things
Such as empires ruled
And the kingdom of kings

All the treasures of life
Would not fill me more
For without this one gift
I'd forever be poor

No greater present
Will I ever see
Than a love I had lost
Come back to me

IF I CAN, SO CAN YOU

Some reach a mountain and see it tall
That mountain, to others, is pretty small
Some think the river is very deep
To some it's just a puddle they can leap

For what we see in life
Will always be
The things which we expect
To always see

If I can cross the river so can you
If I can reach the treetops you can, too
If I can walk my road to the very end
There's no need for you to stop at the bend

If I can see the sunshine it's there for you
If I can hold a moonbeam you can, too
If I can see my life and never be blue
Remember, forever, so can you

WHENEVER

Whenever you're sad and you're feeling blue
Whenever you're lonely and have nothing to do
Whenever you're wishing with feeling so true

Turn to me -
For you know I love you

Whenever you feel life isn't worthwhile
Whenever you have no reason to smile
Whenever the heartache is hurting you, too

Turn to me -
For you know I love you

Whenever you're crying, tears filling your eyes
Whenever you can't see the stars in the skies
Whenever the moon is not smiling for you

Turn to me -
For you know I love you

Forever, my darling, I'll be at your side
Hoping and praying you'll see through your pride
Whenever you want happiness you once knew

Turn to me -
For you know I love you

HOW DO YOU SAY HELLO TO LOVE?

What do I say to that face in the crowd
The face I've so longed to see
How do I tell you, my beautiful one
How much you mean to me

Will I say the words that will make you smile
And share all the world with me
Or will I stumble upon my lips
And make you so fear that you'll flee

What does one say when he sees first his love
God, tell me, what should I do
Should I speak as I've known her forever
Or show her our love is new

I've practiced this moment a thousand times
I've rehearsed it so carefully
But I've forgotten it all, my love
Now that you're here before me

Today we laugh together
Our meeting came naturally
For I forgot to remember
She, too, was looking for me

TEARS OVER NO ONE

Sometime I sit and I stare at the sky
And lonely teardrops come to my eye
I'm thinking of someone I'll never forget
The love meant for me whom I've never met

I think of the years we could've cared
I think of the life we should've shared
I think of the things we would've done
I sit here and think and cry tears over no one

I've spent my whole life never seeing her face
I've spent all my years without her embrace
I've spent all my days never knowing real fun
I've spent all my nights crying tears over no one

Day after day I would sit and I'd pray
For the good Lord in Heaven to show me the way
To know where she was so to her I would run
Instead I sit here and think and cry tears over no one

Should I give up hope? Has life passed me by
Or will I see the day when those tears from my eye
Are wiped away dry by that special someone
Or will I, forever, cry tears -

Over no one

THE BEAUTY OF LIFE

Is the beauty of life:

The sound of a newborn's very first cry
The sun turning night into day
A flower which blooms for the very first time
A lost soul finding its way

Is the beauty of life:

The majestic sound of the Heavenly choir
The first warm day of the spring
The first little sprout of the giant oak tree
The gold, the end of the rainbow, would bring

Is the beauty of life:

The wish we made on a Star coming true
The song of the birds in the morn
The tender touch of a new love's embrace
A love, made in Heaven, been born

No! The beauty of life is:

The treasure God made with His very own hand
Nothing will e'er take its place
The true beauty of life is what my soul sees
When I look at your beautiful face

I CAN IF I LOOK

I'd like to be able to walk up the street
And see smiles on the faces of the people I meet
I'd like to feel all are my friends
A deep, honest friendship which never ends

I'd like to see people speak of happy, not sad
Telling each other life has more good than bad
I'd like to see gestures of love in their way
Spreading its warmth in the world every day

I'd like to see people helping all those in need
Making charity the nutrition on which we all feed
I'd like to see people always giving, not taking
Doing unto others the rule of their making

I'd like to see people doing all these and more
From the moment I step from my home through the door
I'd like to see people as I wish I could see
I can if I look -

For what I see is up to me

WHY DO I LOVE YOU?

Why do I love you; why do I care?
How can you believe my feelings are sincere
Listen to my heart, my love, hear my words so true
This is why, my darling, I know I'm in love with you

I see deep within your eyes the things you cannot hide
I see deep within your soul how you are inside
I see tenderness, compassion, faithfulness, too
I see warmth, understanding, and beauty inside you

I see reverence, peace, the willingness to live
I see years of endless love your heart is eager to give
I also see traces of unhappy days
So too, do I see caution in your ways

I see a woman who wants to be real
But first she must trust what she longs to feel
My words are so true, with love I won't play
I long to fulfill your every day

Let me reach the woman who lies within you
And show her love can be honest and true
I see all the things you've prayed, always, to see
This is why I love you so, please,

Believe in me

THE DREAM FROM GOD

One day when God was resting
His mind began to race
He wanted to create a dream
To be seen in a beautiful face

He started to walk the Heavens
He roamed around the earth
Wherever He passed took with His hand
All things of special worth

He took a ray of the Sun
He took the gleam of a Star
He took the glow from the Moon
And a rainbow from afar

He captured the smoothness of water
And the graceful turn of a hill
Together with softness of flowers
He borrowed the song of a trill

He took all these priceless possessions
And sprinkled them, gently, with dew
So proud was the smile upon His face
When He knew He created you

IT TAKES MORE THAN ONE

The man in the moon wears a wide smile
For he has the Stars to make night time worthwhile
Though the clouds, at times, hide them from sight
They're always together, night after night

Have you ever seen only one drop of rain
Or one flake of snow hit your window pane
They're never alone, always come in a crowd
And they come, always, from more than one cloud

Have you ever seen only one blade of grass
Or a tree with one leaf did you ever pass
Was there ever a beach with one grain of sand
Does one speck of soil make up this great land

Can you make a house with only one wall
Does one brick make a building tall
What good is a table without a chair
What good is a chair if no one sits there

What good is a pen if it has no ink
Have you ever seen a chain with only one link
What good is a song with only one note
Have you ever read a poem with only one word to quote

What good is love; how can one care
If there's no one to love, if there's no one there
What good is one when there should be two
What good am I if there is no you

ALL BECAUSE MY HEART FOUND YOU

My heart came alive at your beautiful sight
You took the loneliness from the night
You awakened my eyes to the beauties of life
You chased, from my heart, despair and strife

I feel again, as a newborn child
Knowing laughter and joy, happiness so wild
The moon is my friend, the stars shine for me
The sun, as your love, brings me warm ecstasy

How wondrous the gift of a new found love
As the flight in the sky of a pure white dove
The branches of trees are waving to me
They're saying how beautiful life really can be

I thought I had lost the smile from my face
But the nearness of you brought it back in its place
Life is so thrilling, excitingly new
And all because my heart found you

SEARCHING

Where have all the good men gone
Is a question asked every day
Are there any decent men in the world
Is what every lady must say

Where have all the ladies gone
Is the other side of the coin
Where are the women who take pride in themselves
Gentlemen ask, when in clusters, they join

What happened to virtue and decency
Where, oh where, has gone self-respect
It appears both sexes must sit home and cry
For they know, "out there", what to expect

I don't know about other women and men
I don't know where they've gone, what they do
All I know, my sweet, lovely one, is

I've spent my life searching for you

AFTER THE MARRIAGE

Yes, I love you, you love me, too
But before we marry, let's talk true
Once you say, "I do thee wed"
Doesn't mean trouble won't share our bed

Many people think the hardest part in life
Is when they try to see if they should be husband and wife
They face all the problems, they conquer all the woe
They struggle through the courtship to try and make it go

They think when they have crossed the deep and churning sea
The two of them will marry and peaceful they will be
That's the biggest error too many people make
They think all is easy after the wedding cake.

It's when two people join and the two become as one
That life presents its problems - they've only just begun
It isn't very hard to catch fish in the sea
It's difficult to know the fish won't slip from me

No one in this world, or even God above
Can ever guarantee a real, true love
Life is full of problems at each and every bend
Don't think marriage brings trouble to an end

So take my hand, walk down the aisle, yes, come and marry me
I'll walk the aisle back with you with a smile for the world to see
But through our married life let's remember, not forget
To never stop trying to win each other yet

Only both of us can make this marriage grow
For if one stops to rest the other will still go
Together we must stay, always, side by side
Ever to each other promise to confide

Speak out each and every problem as small as it may be
For if it's left ignored it can grow gigantically
And let us ne'er forget as long as we shall be
One's problem shared by two is easier to see

And every night before we sleep
Let's get on bended knee
And thank the good Lord up above
For He gave me you and He gave you me

THE PEDESTAL OF GOD

"Come unto Me, My children"
Are the words of God above
"Come unto Me, My little ones
Come and find the joy of love"

"See the Sun that warms the earth
And the Moon of harvest gold
See the Stars which tell the story
Of your love, as yet, untold"

"See the love which lies within you
Crying, truthful, to be free
Find the story of true brotherhood
Which we all wish to see"

"Feel the tenderness, compassion
Which we long, ourselves, to find
Find the truth of truly loving
All ye brothers of mankind"

"Know the wanting to be needed
As the need to need to give
Come unto Me, My children
Come and see the way to live"

"As the dark approaches quickly
Lift your heads to Me and nod
I wait for you, My children
On the pedestal of God"

I'LL ALWAYS REMEMBER YOU

As long as I remember love
I'll always remember you
As long as I remember love
I'll remember the moments we knew

As long as I remember love
And the precious moments we shared
My darling, I'll always remember you
I'll remember how much I cared

As long as there are stars
As long as there's a moon
As long as there is love in the night
And wedding bells in June

As long as there are hearts
Which beat, together, true
As long as I remember love
I'll always remember you

The precious moments we shared
The way you showed me you cared
The feeling you gave to me
The happiness you made me see

The love filled hours we knew
The joy of being with you
The way your lips kissed mine
The way you made life shine

The treasured moments we knew
The feeling of love so true
As long as I remember love
I'll always remember you

HOW DO I KNOW?

You whisper, softly, in my ear,
You tell me things I want to hear.
You touch my check, you kiss my face,
You hold me close in love's embrace.

You run your fingers through my hair,
Anytime and anywhere.
You hold my hand when I feel low,
To make me know,
My fear will go.

You say you're always thinking of me—
But how do I know you really love me?

Because, my darling, you never put—

Anyone else above me!

'SPECIALLY FOR ME

God made the sun,
For everyone.
God made the moon,
For lovers in June.
God made the stars,
For all to see,
But God made my little girl,

'Specially for me.

God made the hills,
For all to climb.
God made night and day,
So there would be time.
God made the angels,
That sing with glee,
But God made my little girl,

'Specially for me.

God made heaven,
Where we'll all be.
God made paradise,
For the good to see.
God made everything,
With love for thee,
But God made my little girl,

'Specially *for me*.

THE ONE YEAR OLD MAN

A very old man was walking the earth
Bedraggled, worn out, he showed no sign of worth
Each slowing step brought more sign of wear
His head, he kept lowered, his eye had a tear

A little boy who was busy at play
Saw the old man and walked his way
The little boy just stood there and stared
Then reached out his hand to show he cared

He said to the old man, "Why cry you today"
The old man answered, "I must go away"

"But before I depart from this world I knew
These words of wisdom I pass on to you
Study them carefully, heed them well
And to all in this world, my words, to them, tell

"Believe though you're poor, you have much wealth
Believe you are rich if you have your health
Believe hate is a word spoken of
Believe the true feeling of man is love

"Believe the word 'stranger' is false, untrue
Believe in brotherhood to all, not a few
Believe in giving all you can
Believe in helping your fellow man

"Believe man's color differs only in sight
Believe the skin is poor reason for fight
Believe despite race, creed, or name
Believe our blood is colored the same

"Believe foreign language differs only to the ear
Believe words not understood are no reason for fear
Believe with whom you live is not yours to decide
Believe your neighbor also has pride

"Believe equality is for not only a few
Believe you're no better and there's no better than you
Believe sadness lasts only a day
Believe happiness fades not away

"Believe most of all in my strongest belief
Believe there's a God and you'll lessen your grief"

"Well, now I've come to my journey's end"
Said the old man as he rounded the bend

The little boy cried, "Sir, your name I didn't hear"

From space came the answer -

"I WAS LAST YEAR'S NEW YEAR"

ONE SENTENCE OF HOPE

A long time ago I read in a book
One sentence of wisdom my memory took
These words were implanted so deep in my mind
They gave me a hope of a life yet to find

For there was a time I was filled with despair
Like millions of others I thought no one would care
In moments of sadness when living seemed vain
I thought of that sentence and hope lived again

I waited and waited for such a long while
For days, weeks, and months, even years, with no smile
Still I recalled those words my mind knew
But often I wondered if they'd ever come true

However, rainfall must stop, clouds blow away
And we open our eyes to that bright, sunny, day
They waiting, as living, goes so very fast
When the waiting becomes a part of our past

That one sentence of wisdom is so very true
That's why I pray it becomes part of you
One sentence of hope which came straight from our Lord

"The longer the wait - the bigger the reward"

THIS IS ALL I ASK

There are times in our lives when we all want to cry
Yet we wear a smile till the sadness goes by
We, all of us, sometime must be as a clown
Showing a smile though our face wants to frown

Our role in life we cannot foresee
And so we act as we think we should be
When things go wrong, as often they do
We hide our hurt and embarrassment, too

It's part of our life and, always, will be
We can't always have the things that we see
But one precious gift, from us, never will leave
The gift of living in make believe

And so from my heart I speak words so dear
My make believe is in holding you near
One favor I ask, though hopeless may seem
Please be as a clown - don't ruin my dream

THIS IS MY BELIEF

The Sun shining brightly every day
Peace and happiness guiding our way
Something pleasant always to say

This is my belief

The world being ruled by only love
The emblem of the world a pure white dove
Love the only thing we think always of

This is my belief

Smiles and laughter on everyone's face
Joy from within setting our pace
Tranquility the sound of the human race

This is my belief

Faith in God our prime possession
Hatred and evil our biggest depression
Acts of decency our only confession

This is my belief

These things and more all coming true
Nothing but good for me and for you
Everyone saying this next line, too

This is my belief

I LOVE YOU, I DO

The first time I met you
I said, "I love you, I do"
You didn't believe those words I said
But, my darling, they really were true

You thought my words were only a joke
You laughed them out of your mind
But you should have looked in my eyes as I spoke
If the truth you wanted to find

I said, "I love you"
And I swear I do
My darling, please believe me

I know I love you
And my love is so true
I hope you will never leave me

The first time I met you
I said, "I love you, I do"
And now I'm saying it over again

"I love you, my darling, I do"

MY THANKS TO GOD

Every day when I awake and the world, again, I see
I give all my thanks to God for all He gave to me
Every time night turns to day I start my life anew
I give all my thanks to God because He gave me you

I thank my Lord, my God above, for good things I can do
But I thank Him most of all because He gave me you

I thank Him for the flowers
I thank Him for the trees
I thank Him for the grass so green
I thank Him for the seas

I thank Him for the friends I have
The old ones and the new
But I thank Him most of all
Because He gave me you

I thank Him for the people whom I meet every day
I thank Him for the smiles I see and the nice words they say
I thank Him for the miracles He, alone, can do
I thank Him for the blessings I have He gave with love so true

I thank my Lord, my God above, as I look at the sky so blue
And I thank God with all my heart -

Because He gave me you!

THE SADDEST WORD

The saddest word I'll ever hear
It's always accompanied by a tear
It's the end of a life, the end of a day
The start of a blue, unhappy, way

It's so hard to say when it comes from the heart
For it means it's the time of a final depart
It opens the door of the memories of your mind
It makes you re-live the days no more to find

It makes your future uncertain, your life sad and blue
It destroys all the plans, all the things left to do
It makes you wonder where all went wrong
And you feel as though you don't belong

You close your eyes, pray to start again
With what you know now and you wish you knew then
But yesterday's gone, won't come back anymore
For you never can open a tightly closed door

So for the rest of your life you stare at the sky
Recalling the day your loved one said -

Good-by

YOUR MEMORY

I lost your embrace
The sight of your face
Your love was taken from me

But never my darling
Will I ever lose
Your beautiful memory

The days are all gone
When you were mine
Our dreams are never to be

Your heart went astray
You walked away
But with me stays your memory

My heart yearns for
What is no more
My future with you
I won't see

You left my side
Left a void so wide
But you left me your memory

Day by day I sit and I pray
I pray ever so faithfully
That you'll come back into my life
in place of your memory

THE RIGHT TIME AND PLACE

I never knew your love
I never felt its warm embrace
For though it was the right time
I was always in the wrong place

I never saw your smile
Or the glow within your eye
I never heard your lovely voice
Because, my darling, I
Was never where you were
At that precious moment sublime

It always turned out to be -

The wrong place or the wrong time

My darling, was it meant
Forever more to be
That I would never be
Where you'd be next to me

If I'd walked a little slower
Or maybe a little fast
All those lonely days I've spent
Wouldn't be part of my past

For maybe I would've found you
Enjoyed the love on your face
If, my darling, it would have been

The right time and place

REMEMBER THE FLOWER

Not so long ago when our love was very new
We did all the things all true lovers do
We walked hand in hand, along the path of love
Thankful for the happiness we thought always of

Our love was like the flowers you see upon the hill
The Rose, Gardenia, Violet and the pretty Daffodil
As they, we bloomed from day to day because of love so true
The flower became our symbol of love and
the happy moments we knew

Oh, my darling, Oh, my love, all the flowers that I gave
You cherished every petal as our true love to save
We were living in a garden only two of us had shared
We never ceased to tell each other how much we really cared

Now, my darling, years have passed and with them we did change
The life we lived so long ago began to re-arrange
The love which was so tall and strong is starting now to cower
Think back, my love, think back to the past
My darling, remember the flower?

MY THOUGHT

To be with you
My entire life through
Is the only thing I pray

To share with you
A love so true
I pray for day after day

To say you're mine
To live flowers and wine
Is the only wish I seek

To walk in the sun
Together as one
I wish for week after week

To have your heart
Never to part
Is the hope I hold so dear

To make my life whole
Feel your love in my soul
I hope for year after year

To walk down the aisle
Sharing your smile
Dreaming you'll be my wife

To know you will be
Mine eternally
I dream every night of my life

UNTIL COMES THAT DAY

I've waited and waited so patiently
For the day to come when you'd come back to me
But the will of my God is very plain
All of my waiting has been in vain

I can see, now, tomorrow will be as today
And today is as every yesterday
The dreams, the hopes, I've prayed always for
Will fade from my mind though not evermore

If ever again though our paths should cross
The sight of you will bring back my loss
The pain I feel now I will feel then again
And the love I'll show will be twice as strong then

Your memory will live in the back of my mind
So the sweet taste of love, at times, I might find
And when I grow old and my head becomes white
I'll call forth those memories every night

Then the joy, the happiness, I've lived in the past
Will stay beside me forever to last
Until comes that day when I'll no longer be
Your memory will always live within me

NOW I KNOW

One thing I've learned in my life on earth
I've seen it over and over since the day of my birth
At first I gave it very little thought
But as I grew older I saw what it brought

In the days of my youth I tried to arrange
The things in my life which I couldn't change
I tried, very hard, to set my own course
And those times I failed were filled with remorse

When things went well I was filled with pride
For I thought the outcome was mine to decide
When things went wrong I was angry at fate
And my mind and my soul filled, quickly, with hate

When I was a winner I held my head high
When I was a loser I wished I would die
I sat and I thought of where I went wrong
And I placed the blame where it didn't belong

But now I'm older, I see everything clear
And my knowledge diminished most of my fear
I've learned the lesson of life, the most important one
I've come to believe - God's will be done

MY TRUE FRIENDS

My life saw times good
My life saw times bad
As with everyone else
I've seen happy and sad

I've had many a friend
When life went well
The number dwindled
When I was in hell

I reached my hand out
To people I saw
There were those who took it
And there were those who'd ignore

There were many who said
I'd no longer be
There were those who showed
They had faith in me

I'm an average man
Important, I'm not
But I'm rich when I'm with
Those who never forgot

My life has been bless'd
With friends so true
And this is my poem
Saying, *"I truly love you"*

I'LL FORGET TO THINK OF YOU

When the sun no longer shines
And the moon fades from my view
Only then, my darling
I'll forget to think of you

When the stars no longer glow
And the clouds stop rolling, too
Only then, my darling
I'll forget to think of you

For your memory lives within me
In the shadow of my mind
No longer will I find
A love so pure and kind

I still think so deeply of you
I remember our love so true
And the picture of your face
Is burned deeply in my mind

When the world no longer turns
And the days are but a few
Only then, my darling
I'll forget to think of you

IMPORTANT CONVERSATION

An honest conversation for a husband and a wife
Is the most important factor in a happily married life
It's a way to let your feelings open very wide
For a marriage can be ruined if all is kept inside

A conversation is, and always will be
A way of relating all that we see
No two people always see things the same
A quiet conversation eliminates all blame

Sometime one person will live their life in stress
Then the other partner will offer to suggest
For it's always been true and forever will be
What we cannot see ourselves the other one can see

But an honest conversation will always be a waste
If one or the other speaks in thoughtless haste
No one expects decisions without careful thought
For an answer that's not slept on will always be for naught

But remember, forever, as you both sit down to speak
Outside influences will tend to make you weak
Think for one another, always put your partner first
And all throughout your married life, for love, you'll never thirst

Feelings of guilt, or of hurting other people
Can make a marriage fall like a crumbling steeple
If they really love you as they always say they do
No matter how you live your life they'll know it's best for you

WHENEVER I'M HOLDING YOU

The Heavens resound with a thunderous roar
As the lightning streaks from shore to shore
The wind travels quickly and veers as one cue
Whenever, my darling, I'm holding you

The trees come alive and spread arms so wide
The flowers bloom as they dance side to side
The world becomes foggy with misty dew
Whenever, my darling, I'm holding you

Angels start singing in voices so loud
As they graciously prance from cloud to cloud
The moon and the stars quickly come into view
Whenever, my darling, I'm holding you

But to me all is quiet, and peaceful, and calm
I feel not a quake as you rest in my arm
Oblivious, I, to the happenings true
Whenever, my darling, I'm holding you

IT WAS THEN I KNEW

It wasn't on the second day
It wasn't on the third day
It wasn't on the fourth day I knew

No, my darling
It was on the first day

I fell in love with you

It wasn't at second sight
It wasn't at third sight
It wasn't at fourth sight I knew

No, my darling
It was on the first kiss

I knew you loved me, too

It wasn't on the second kiss
It wasn't on the third kiss
It wasn't on the fourth kiss I knew

No, my darling
It was on the first kiss

I knew you loved me, too

It wasn't the second time
It wasn't the third time
It wasn't the fourth time I knew

No, my darling
It was every time

I knew I'd forever love you

WHY? WHY NOT?

There comes a time we must accept the happenings
of life without question

Smart men know the answers to everything

Wise men know everything to answer

Would the flower smell any the sweeter if we knew
how, and why, the flower came to be

Would a newborn babe be loved, any the more,
if the miracle of birth were fully understood

Do we question the existence of a tree

If there were no mysteries, where would be the
excitement of life

I seek not the answer . . . I need not the answer

I know, only, you and I were brought together

That, to me, is the answer of life

That, to me, is the epitome of life

How do I love -
Why do I love -
I needn't know

I only know
I love

I know

I love you

WHERE IS GOD?

Many people constantly ask
Why God hears not their prayer
They sit alone and wonder
If God is really there

They look at those around them
And see those lives are bless'd
Then they turn and say to God
"Why not treat 'me' like the rest"

And so they live their lives
As though they were alone
Saying "God's too busy for me
Up there on His Heavenly throne"

They turn to other people
And raise their heads up high
"I don't believe in God", they say
"I can't see Him with my eye"

They live their lives as they so choose
They do whatever they please
They have no worry or fear of sin
All the comforts of life they seize

But then when trouble befalls them
They run and they pray to God
Saying, "God, please comfort me
Thou art my Staff and Rod"

People as this take long to learn
Their ways are small and slim
For you must seek God every day of your life
More so when you *don't* need Him

THIS POEM

I'm writing this poem
To let you know
I think constantly of you
Wherever I go

I'm writing this poem
So I can say
You're on my mind
Every day

I'm writing this poem
So you can feel
It's your beautiful heart
I'm trying to steal

I'm writing this poem
So you can see
Forever and ever
You're part of me

Every word of this poem
Is honestly true
And I wrote this poem
Because I love you

MY CHILDREN

There is no greater blessing from the Lord above
Than the children He made for me to give love
For the rest of my days, wherever I'll be
I will cherish the children God gave to me

Without their sweet voices to hear every day
A meaningless life would be my only way
Their innocence reigns as they lie fast asleep
My love for their being is instilled in me deep

With these thoughts in mind, my Heavenly King
Please, give me the patience of the angels who sing
In those times of my life when I act as a fool
Please remind me to heed each and every rule:

I will never forget my children are young
And loudly the songs of their youth must be sung
I will never forget they have energy untold
And this strength in children must daily unfold

I will never forget they don't know right from wrong
And these teachings of life are lessons so long
I will never forget my children can't see danger
And always need the guidance of a constant re-arranger

I will never forget young eyes which still weep
Take a very long time to fall off to sleep
I will never forget they have limited sight
And it's natural for children to fight day and night

I will never forget the eager road they take
And what stands in their way they'll constantly break
I will never forget as through parenthood I plod
My children are blessings - given me by God

THE GIRL I'M GOING TO MARRY

She wears ribbons and bows
And conservative clothes

The girl I'm going to marry

Her hair is so shiny
Her feet are so tiny

The girl I'm going to marry

She'll never displace the smile on her face
A frown she never will carry
Her cheeks are so rosy
Her eyes warm and cozy

The girl I'm going to marry

And when she speaks
Her mouth just wreaks
Of the love which comes from her heart

I love her so madly
I give myself gladly
From her, I never would part

I always will love her
I'll think always of her
She means more to me than my life

I always will love her
I'll place no one above her

The girl who will be my dear wife

IT'S RAINING WITH
NO RAINDROPS

It's raining with no raindrops
In the sky
All the raindrops that I see
Are in my eye

Yes, it's raining and it's pouring
Lightning's streaking
Thunder's roaring
And it's raining with no raindrops in the sky

My true blue skies above
Have turned to gray
Will I ever see another sunny day

Oh, the lightning is so frightening
Floods are flooding
Clouds are tightening

And it's raining with no raindrops
In the sky

My true love went away
And left me blue
There's only one thing left
That I can do

I can only keep on sighing
While my eyes go right on crying
And it's raining with no raindrops in the sky

THE UNANSWERABLE QUESTION

I pace the room, walk here and there
I run my fingers through my hair
I think of the do's, I think of the don'ts
I weigh the will's, I question the won'ts

I talk to myself; I answer back
I wonder why, my nerves, I wrack
I search my mind, I look for a clue
I reach a decision, I decide it won't do

I sit in a chair; I tap my fingers
I try to forget, yet, the question still lingers
I look at the phone, temptation is great
That's the wrong thing to do, I'd better wait

I sit by the window, I stare at the sky
I talk to the stars which twinkle on high
I close my eyes, I say a prayer
Hoping to find the answer there

Time's moving on, it's getting late
Maybe I'll leave it up to fate
No, I have to find the answer tonight
For if I don't I won't sleep alright

I take a deep breath; I pick up the phone
My hand starts to shake as I hear the dial tone
I hang up the phone; I let things be
Tomorrow I'll ask her - *Do you love me?*

WHAT TIME IS LOVE?

Love in the morning
Love in the evening
Love in the afternoon

Love on the weekday
Love on the weekend
Love never comes too soon

Love in the summer
Love in the Winter
Love in the springtime, too

Love in the fall
Anytime at all
Love is for me and for you

Love, love, plenty of love
Love when the sun shines bright
Love, love, plenty of love
Even in the dark of night

Love, love, plenty of love
Underneath the shining moon
Love, love, plenty of love
In January or in June

Love, love, the whole year through
Summer, Winter, Spring or Fall
Love, love, let's make love
Darling, anytime at all

WHAT IS LOVE?

What is it that makes a person know love?
What is that magical power?
Why do I think of a certain someone
Hour after hour?

Why do my thoughts go never astray
But stay always on one so dear?
Why does my world revolve around one
Whether far away or near?

What is it that makes my body yearn
For that special someone I see?
What is the formula known as love
Which lives deep within you and me?

Why do I long to be, always, by
That one in a million face?
Why is it there is only one
Who makes my heart start to race?

I can't explain the reason for love
I don't know why I feel as I do
I only know it's alive within me
And all because of you

CHERISH YOUR MEMORIES

Those times when you sit and think of the past
Don't remember them as times that just couldn't last
There were good times and bad times and times that were mixed
Arrange all those memories though they feel firmly fixed

The good things remembered, though gone, make us cry
We recall every moment as still seen with our eye
Don't feel depressed for the good gone away
Cherish those memories as your bright, happy day

The bad things remembered may fill us with hate
But what good is hating when now it's too late
Remember the bad, push them not from your mind
They're the lessons of life which we're lucky to find

Memories mixed, don't try to make clear
They cause feelings of guilt for their truth may bring fear
Why try to decide who's to blame for the past
We would've known then had our thoughts ran not fast

Cherish your memories, however they seem
Be thankful you have them, they're your basis for dream
Experience comes from this life which we live
For without this true knowledge, what have we to give

IF A BIRD IN THE SKY, WERE I

I wish I could fly
As a bird in the sky
I'd fly o'er the sea and the land

I'd fly o'er the mountains
I'd fly o'er the trees
And the burning, hot desert of sand

I'd fly through the cloud
And the storm in the night
No form of nature to trap me

I'd fly high and low
Ever forward I'd go
Being so very happy

I'd fly through the cold
I'd fly fierce and bold
I'd fly till my body grew weary

I'd fly up and down
I'd fly all around
And sorrow would never be near me

I'd fly and I'd fly
I'd fly till I die
I'd fly and I never would cry

I'd fly and I'd fly
I'd fly ever so high
If a bird in the sky, were I

GOD STILL LOVES ME

My days were dark, my nights very blue
More often than always there was nothing to do
Tears in my eyes were my way of life
My echo of living, despair and strife

Every night before sleep would befall
I'd ask God in Heaven why He heard not my call
Unanswered my prayers were destined to be
Impossible seemed beauty for my eyes to see

Each driving day caused more ache in my heart
With each crying night my wish further would part
My laughter was lessened; hopes dwindled to few
My dreams, very quickly, were diminishing, too

But then as a ray of the sun in the morn
My life became bright, once again I was born
The beauty of living came back unto me
God granted the miracle I prayed so to see

He proved my waiting had not been in vain
He proved the Sunshine does follow the rain
He proved the gray skies do turn to blue
He proved He still loves me - *when He gave me you*

IT HAS TO BE FOR LOVE

Today I took a star from out of the sky
I placed it on a flower that stood so high
I closed my eyes and I said a prayer
When I opened my eyes you were there

Your eyes and your hair were shining so bright
They offered more beauty than the moon in the night
Your body was soft as the flower's own petal
Your fragrance, so calmly, made my mind settle

I reached out to hold you but you stepped away
A tear from your eye turned my blue sky to gray
I reached out again but once more you swayed
I became confused, completely dismayed

I looked to the Heavens, I quickly asked why
I could only hold you by the sight of my eye
A little bird flew and landed on my shoulder
And whispered to me softly, "This is why you cannot hold her"

After the secret was said in my ear
I turned to see if you were still near
I said, "I'm sorry for not thinking true"
And you came into my arms when I said, "*I love you*"

LIFE'S TREASURES

Life's treasures are:

- The Sun in the sky
- The twinkling Stars
  - A tall tree
  - A soft flower
  - A blade of grass
  - A blue sky
  - A white cloud
  - A Sunset
  - A friendly hello
  - A warm smile
  - A handshake
  - A kiss
  - A caress
  - A warm touch
  - A gentle word
  - A tender look

And -

You!

THE VOICES OF HEAVEN

Heaven speaks in many ways
Its voices are heard both nights and days
Every little sound that you may hear
Is Heaven speaking in ways so clear

The sweet, tender melody of the babbling brook
Holds more conversation than is found in a book
It's telling you words of calm and peace
Soft music to your ears which never will cease

The rustling of the branches on the swaying tree
Is Heaven playing a symphony
The soft, tender, crackle of the leaves on the ground
Reminds you that Heaven is all around

The strong, majestic voice of the swirling waterfall
Is telling you of Heaven's love; so high, so large, so tall
The roaring of the rapids as they move swiftly by
Reminds you there's more to life, more than meets the eye

The sound of crunching pebbles on every path you make
Is the voice of Heaven guiding you with every step you take
And even when it's still, no sound to meet the ear
That's the quiet sound of Heaven's voice reminding you it's there

WHY DO WE FAIL?

When life is lonely and sad and blue
We pray to God in Heaven for love so true
We kneel in prayer most every night
For someone to free us from our plight

We promise our Lord in Heaven above
We'll be worthy and thoughtful to our new love
We solemnly pledge when for love we thirst
The needs and the wants of the other come first

And then one day our wish we receive
We think it's a dream for it's hard to believe
God answered our prayer; He didn't forget
We're so happy to know He loves us yet

Then together we go on our merry way
Making plans and promises every day
The mistakes of the past we'll never repeat
This love will never do down in defeat

With problems resolved and with eyes opened wide
We promise, forever, to live side by side
We've spoken so deeply, erased all doubt
Now we must practice what we've spoken about

We can change our ways, for each other can live
Prove to each other we truly can give
Hand in hand through this life we can sail
Or once again ask, *"Why Do We Fail"*

CLOSE YOUR EYES AND SEE

In moments of sadness when cry I must
I take comfort in knowing there's one I can trust
To take all my burdens and set my mind free
And one does exist who does this for me

Forever and ever He's there at my side
Waiting to help if I ask with no pride
He'll turn never from me for not even one day
He stays constantly with me though I walk away

It took a long time for me to find Him
Though His presence was glowing my mind made Him dim
With patience and reverence He waited for me
For somehow He knew one day I would see

How foolish the years I lived in pure waste
Not feeling Him near as I ran with such haste
When finally I found Him it was a surprise
For He cannot be seen if you look with your eyes

Strangely enough His presence is here
If you'll close your eyes you'll see Him near
Don't run, don't search, look not above
For God is beside you if you want his love

FAILING IS WINNING

Too many of us sit in despair
We feel we're defeated and winning is rare
We rationalize the thoughts in our mind
We say we're born losers and fate's been unkind

We attempt to reach the Moon set afar
Or capture a rainbow or touch a Star
We set our sights to the top of the hill
Then we find our dreams we cannot fulfill

We lose our loved ones, they're taken away
We sit in self pity; drown with dismay
We try to reach success in our field
If we don't succeed to frustration we yield

Then we think, forever, we're living in hell
And many of us withdraw in a shell
There's no use in trying, we say all hope is lost
For the price of failure is too high a cost

But what is a failure, what makes one lose
Not having conquered the feats which we choose?
No, losing is winning, fate has not lied
You're a born winner - because you have tried

WHO IS TO SAY?

Many a day we spend with fear
For trouble and sickness seem so near
We exaggerate within our mind
Convince ourselves the worst we'll find

This negative thought is hard to suppress
And only because we fail to confess
To admit what we know and yet what we do
We fear only fear and it's so very true

If we close our eyes and go back in time
We'll remember the past wasn't always sublime
Hardship and worry, despair and strife
Were present in other times in our life

But did we succumb in those days of the past
Was every anxiety always the last
No, the answer we see is very plain
Most of our fears were all in vain

The only thing we're afraid of today
Is the law of averages to which we must pay
We've set in our head this time it is real
And it's not in our mind this thing we feel

But the law of averages works two ways
The scale must balance one of these days
So why go on thinking the worst is here
For what we may lose, forever, is fear

THE BEAUTY OF FREEDOM

To be free as the wind
Unkept as the sun
To walk with no shackles
Be hindered by none

To feel as the bird
Which flies in the sky
In the free spacious vast
Seen as far as the eye

To know barriers not
As the clear desert sand
All the beauty of nature
To reach with your hand

To hear life's sweet song
With no noise to the ear
So soothing, refreshing
Romantically clear

To be free of all bonds
Of the body and soul
Yes, the beauty of freedom
A dream to behold

HOW RICH IS A RICH MAN

A man may be wealthy
Have riches untold
Own wells of oil
Mines of silver and gold

He may dwell in mansions
Own acres of land
Fortunes of money
He may hold in his hand

Yachts and ships
A rich man could buy
Airplanes galore
Could be his to fly

All the power of money
May make him feel strong
And bring him comfort
His entire life long

But how rich is he
This man we think of
How rich is he
If he never knew love

TRUE LOVE IS KNOWING

When you love someone your love is so deep
The nearness of them you strive, always, to keep
You want ever to see their beautiful face
Keep their head on your shoulder in love's sweet embrace

To hold the hands of the ones you love dear
To stay by their side showing how much you care
Is the way of revealing the love inside you
Is so pure, so honest, so tall, so true

You want, especially, in times of their grief
To take all their burdens, let them sigh with relief
You are willing to walk through the fires of hell
In hopes your loved ones forever stay well

Your very own life you'd give, gladly, away
To know your loved ones may smile one more day
You'd barter with God in Heaven above
To give you their pain, let your loved ones live love

Yes, the way of true love, many ways, is shown
Our loved one's happiness we place over our own
And that's why, my darling, I want you to know
A true deep love also - *is knowing when to let go*

MY ONLY WISH

It's so nice to have a family
And a home so full of love
That's the only thing I pray for
When I pray to God above

Every day and every night
I kneel on bended knee
And bow my head and ask the Lord
To give these things to me

It's my only way of living
The way to spend my life
A beautiful home and family
With a thoughtful, loving, wife

So many happy children
True products of our love
Home, children, and each other
What we think always of

Add to this a dog
And a tank of pretty fish
My dream of life is now complete
My dream, my only wish

LOVE

Love is not felt only in the heart

Love is not felt only in the soul

Love is a product of one's entire being

The whole body reacts to love

Beauty is seen, darkness disappears

Every day begins with the tender juices of happiness
flowing throughout our entire being

Things taken for granted, now, are seen clearly
when there is love

The smiles are seen

Frowns are non-existent

All our senses come alive where once they lay dormant
in a state of lovelessness

We experience a strong desire to create

We sing

We dance

There is no such thing as pain - when there is love

In love we forget one person - ourself

Our thoughts are constantly attuned to the needs
and wants of our beloved

In love there is a strong sense of security

In love life seems eternal

In love we are in Heaven

In love there is a strength within us which
we knew not existed

In love we are different

We are new

But the most important result of love is the
non-controllable factor -

-All signs of love are automatic

- They cannot be turned off at will

Poets, for centuries, have attempted to define love

The definition has always been there -

Love is you!

WHAT IS THE PAST?

I sometime sit and think of the past

What is the past?

The yesterday re-named today?

Is the past as the melting snow - gone from sight?

Or does the past remain in the night?

Is a new snowfall - a future past?
Are the falling leaves - a life past?

But the snows and the leaves are, again, to be

What is the past?

The present and the future come and gone?

Do I re-live the past?
Have I walked this way before?

What is time?
How is time measured?

By man's innovation?

If not for the clock or the calendar -
Would there be a yesterday?
Would there be a tomorrow?
Would today be always?

God gives man the day - Man gives day a number

What is the past?

I speak -

- I say the present is now

This word, "now", was uttered in the time gone by

Where is the present?
What is the past?

A breeze kisses my face - yet has kissed another's
in its journey

Do I re-live another's past?

The sounds I hear were heard by another -
-seconds - moments - before

What is the present?

What is the future?

What is the past?

What is the past?

What is the past????

MY TRUE LOVE WAITS FOR ME

Somewhere over the mountains
Across the deep blue sea
Somewhere far beyond
My true love waits for me

Across the burning desert
Over the endless land
Somewhere in the distance
She waits with open hand

I'll climb the highest mountain
I'll swim the deepest sea
I'll crawl the burning desert
Till my loved one stands with me

I'll fly against the strongest wind
I'll walk in the pouring rain
I'll travel with the lightning
Over the meadow and plain

I'll never cease to wander
Forever I will roam
I'll never end my journey
Till my heart has found its home

Somewhere over the mountains
Across the deep blue sea
Somewhere far beyond
My true love waits for me

Across the burning desert
Over the endless land
Somewhere in the distance
She waits with open hand

THE SIGN OF THE CROSS

My God, my King, my Saviour above
Was nailed to a cross because He preached love
He looked to Heaven as His last breath He drew
And said, "Forgive them, Father, they know not what they do"

For centuries, now, the Cross is our sign
Our way of communicating with the Divine
The Sign of the Cross precedes all our prayer
To ever remind us God is still here

The Sign of the Cross is a motion so small
Yet its meaning is endless, eternally tall
The Cross is our life; The Cross is our way
The Sign of the Cross should start man's every day

The Father, The Son, The Holy Spirit of Love
The Master, The Earth Form, The pure White Dove
Three beings in one, the Holy Trinity
The most Sacred of Sacred, the ultimate Divinity

Whatever your faith, however you love
Remember, forever, the words from above
"There is only one God, forgetting Him is your loss"
So, in your own special way, make the Sign of the Cross

WHAT A SON IS TO ME

The beauty of nature for all to see
Is exactly described by people like me
But words can't be written by anyone
Which can fully explain the meaning of "Son"

It's one thing in life a man must live
For the description of "Son" no one can give
I've tried and I've tried as hard as can be
To put into words what a Son is to me

I can't put on paper the feeling of pride
I cannot relate the love felt inside
I'll never find ways, till the day I die
To simulate the feeling of "my Son and I"

I can only tell you the things I see
Then try to imagine what goes on in me

I see a boy with a dirty face
Is he really part of the human race?
His hair is messy; his shirt has a tear
He has scratches and bumps here and there
His shoes are untied; his socks are torn
He didn't look that way when he was born
His pants are ragged, a hole in the knee
Gee, I'm pretty sure he belongs to me

A baseball cap in his pocket, rolled tight
His eye looks like he just caught a right
But still to me he brings feelings of joy
For whatever he looks like, that's my boy

Yesterday he drove a train
The day before he flew a plane
Last week he was a spaceman, too
Tomorrow God knows what he'll do
But I let him be what he wants to be
As long as I know he belongs to me
And what do they matter, these dreams he's had
He'll still come over and say, "Hi, dad"

I remember the time he climbed a tree
And he yelled out loud "Hey, Dad, look at me"
Then he showed me how good he could skate
And for the rest of the day he stood up when he ate
Then that time in the park when he hit a home run
I looked at the crowd and I said, "That's my Son!"

I remember the times most of all
When my Son would say, "Dad, you wanna play ball"

Yes, a Son is a Son. He's a Dad's pride and joy
A Son is a father's own little boy
A Son gives a man a reason to live
My Son gave me all there was to give

God showed me how strong His love can be
When He made my Son and He gave him to me

I SEE

When I rest my head and I close my eyes
Such beautiful sights I see
I see all the things I've wanted to see
I see all of these things before me:

I see peace and harmony in the world
I see people who are happy to live
I see man helping man in all walks of life
I see everyone eager to give

I see everyone wearing a smile on their face
I see everyone brimming with love
I see everyone lifting their eyes to the sky
Giving thanks to Heaven above

I see nothing but strength in all those around
I see sickness a thing of the past
I see lonely, and hatred, and grief in the world
All gone, all too weak to last

I see all the beauty of living on earth
I see all I wished things would be
I see all that man, for ages, has dreamed

Then I open my eyes and I see . . . ??????

THE STORY OF HEAVEN

The children were restless, lie awake in their bed
This happens when questions go around in their head
I walked in and sat, to each gave a kiss
Their problems were heavy, they went something like this:

"What is the Sun for?" Regina said
"That's the kitchen of Heaven where angels make bread"
"Why is there a Moon?" Michael implied
"That's the night light of Heaven when all are inside"

"Why are there Stars?" Steven did ask
"Some angels work nights, carry lights for their task"
"I'll bet you don't know why there's clouds" Robbie said
"For the angels to sleep, that's their soft, fluffy bed"

"And the rain we have when the angels shower
The flakes of snow, their after bath powder
The thunder is when God wants to be heard
The lightning's the path where He'll speak His word"

"And after the meeting of those up above
Their applause brings us wind, they heard God's love
And when the sky's dark, no light to be seen
That's a holiday in Heaven by Mary, the Queen"

"That's the story of Heaven for children to keep
Now, turn around, close your eyes, go off to sleep"

THOSE GOLDEN DAYS

Sometime I think of those days gone by
Those days which are now endless times in the sky
Those days are remembered for their good, not their bad
For we tend to remember the happy, not the sad

Those times I would sit by the radio
And close my eyes as I listened to the show
The chillers, the thrillers, the comedies, too
The hours of music played by a talented few

The records which would break if you dropped them on the floor
The piano in the parlor with rolls of paper that played the score
The vaudeville show in the neighborhood movie house
The prizes at the door given to many a man's spouse

The half a day spent at the local movie show
Watching movie after movie where for ten cents I would go
The king sized, jumbo, five cent candy bar
The ride back home on the three cent trolley car

The two cent stamp; the penny post card
The mail that came two times a day by mailmen who would nod
The newspaper which, for two cents, I would buy
The nickel ice cream cone, two tiers high

The ice cream parlor - The corner candy store
The joyful hours spent sitting outside our front door
The times people sat together in the park
For hours and hours on the bench after dark

The cop on the beat with the big, heavy stick
Who was allowed to break up each and every clique
The clicking sound of the milkman's horse
The large blocks of ice the iceman would toss

The little old man selling peanuts from the cart
The good old Charlotte Rousse - The home made pastry tart
The ten cent ice cream soda - The five cent tall egg cream
Candy stuck on paper - Empty bottles to redeem

The cobbler working hard to make our shoes look new
The butcher taking out the bone before weighing meat for you
The little children playing marbles in the dirt
Little girls and women always wearing a dress or a skirt

The two dollar visit for a checkup every fall
The three dollar fee for the doctor's house call

Many, many, memories I'll never see again
But never will my mind forget those golden days of then

MY MIND DIDN'T TELL MY HEART

My love was as deep as the ocean blue
My entire world revolved around you
We were made for each other; we two were as one
The life we lived could come never undone

As the rays from the sun, my love glowed on you
As the twinkle of stars, my heart beat so true
As the glow of the moon casts its magical hue
My heart and my soul loved you more than you knew

My body would shiver as you came into sight
I yearned to be near you night after night
My dreams you captured; my thoughts you enslaved
Every part of my being for you, constantly, craved

But now I'm without you; my world turns no more
You left me in darkness when you closed the door
Deep down inside I knew we would part
My eyes told my mind - but my mind -

Didn't tell my heart

TEACH ME TO FORGET

Teach me how to say good-bye
To the happy memory
Show me how I can forget
What meant the world to me

Teach me how to stop the dreams
Of the happy, carefree day
Show me how I can erase
Those times which went away

Tell me how to stop the day
From turning into night
Tell me how to stop the birds
From flying in the sky

Can you stop the grass from growing
Can you make the tree stand still
Can you stop the sun from shining
Can you hold back time until -

You teach me how to say good-bye
To the happy memory
Show me how I can forget
What meant the world to me

I REMEMBER

I remember those days when I held you in my arms
I remember the times I shared your sweet loving charms
I remember the way your eyes stared at mine so
I remember your sparkle, your glimmer, your glow

    The way you sat very close to me
    Your hand in mine resting on my knee
    And on my shoulder lay your beautiful head
    The tears of joy your happy eyes shed

    The warmth, the love, that kept us bound
    The true, happy love we knew we had found
    The words of endearment that rang out so true
    Your love vowed to me - my love vowed to you

    The promises made from the depth of our heart
    That forever, and ever, we never would part

I remember those days as they passed on and on
I remember those days though those days are now gone
I remember those times, I will never forget
I remember you, my darling, I remember you yet

A SONG FOR YOU AND ME

The stars shone bright throughout the night
The moon was there to see
The angels sang a song on high
A song for you and me

The sun caressed the morning dew
The clouds rolled joyfully
The trees sang softly in the wind
A song for you and me

The flowers burst and came alive
The grass waved like the sea
The rooster sang a song in tune
A song for you and me

Now we sing our song of love
We sing for eternity
The song that singing songs will sing
A song for you and me

GIVE IT AWAY

It's warm; it's tender; it's a wondrous sight
It helps to brighten the darkest night
It's the gift of gifts though entirely free
It's the treasure of life for all people to see

If you pass it around the loss is not known
For it's quickly by those to whom it's shown
It cannot be kept or saved for a day
For as it's received it's given away

It cannot be hidden; cannot be disguised
For it's passed on to others before realized
It cannot be lost or left far behind
For whenever you leave it, another you'll find

So always give yours to people in need
They will take it and return it with no sign of greed
You'll find your life is very worthwhile
If you constantly give your warm, friendly smile

MY SON

From the day you were born you were special to me
You were all in the world, what more could there be
You were handsome and strong, my pride and joy
Yes, you were my son, my little boy

We played together; had so much fun
There's no greater team than father and son
The two of us, always, side by side
My head held high, my chest filled with pride

We played baseball, football, basketball, too
We did all the things men like to do
We sat together and watched the pro's play
I dreamed you would be one some day

Yes, you were my son, a man to me
Yet my little boy you always would be
For when things went wrong and problems you had
You'd always say, "Can I talk to you, Dad"

Nothing God made could ever replace
The look of joy that came to your face
When, together we made your problems small
My God, that made me ten feet tall

Yes, my son, you filled my life so
I'll never know why you had to go
After all the things we planned would be
How could God let you be taken from me

My life now is empty; so lonely and sad
For I can't hear your voice calling me "Dad"
But forever and ever till my life is done
The night carries my words, *"I love you, my son"*

CHILDREN OF LOVE

I went inside my children's room and sat upon the bed
The children turned and spoke to me; I
was shocked by what they said
"We want to hear a story, Dad, but not of make believe
We want to know where we came from
and what it means to conceive"

I quickly sat back on the bed; my mind was working fast
I knew I'd hear that question soon, now here it was at last
I told them all to gather around and listen carefully
They jumped up like a jack-in-the-box and sat in front of me

"God made man and woman from the love within His heart
He joined them together as husband and
wife so never they would part
He said to them:
'Now walk the earth, walk wherever you please
Walk in the meadow; walk in the field; walk amongst the tree
And as you walk this land together, one thing I want you to see
See all my creations on this earth; see how they all please me'

'See how the tree brings all its beauty to the earth
See how the fruit of the tree gives the tree its worth
Look upon the seed of the fruit of the tree
See the seed fall into the earth so another tree will be'

'See the seed of the flower as the flower bends its head
To bring forth more flowers, the flower's seed is shed
All those things are done especially for me
The seed is a symbol of love so for me more life will be'

'So it is with animals of which man is also known
To bring forth more children so more love for me is shown
The seed of reproduction from true love is received
As it's nurtured between husband and wife, this is called *conceived*"

"So, my children, now you see you come from a great big love
The love between your mommy and me
and the love from God above"

THE GIFT FROM GOD

God took a flower
God took a tree
God took some sunshine
He took some of the sea

God took a rainbow from the sky so blue
He kissed them lightly and there was you

God took the music from angels above
God plucked a feather from a dove
God took the moonlight, the starlight, too
He kissed them lightly and there was you

When he was finished; His day's work done
He said to His Mother, "Here's a special one"
Then the Heavens sang with songs of glee
As He turned around and gave you to me

WHEN PATHS CROSS

Every person who lives alone
Prays to God every day
"Please dear Lord", the voice rings out
"To my love help me find the way"

During our wait we constantly stare
With envy at others we see
We feel the world is passing us by
And we say, "There's no hope for me"

The days and nights just pass right on by
At times we feel tired of living
It's during these moments, when we feel low
We accuse God of taking, not giving

Then as fast the lightning which streaks from the sky
The day we prayed for arrives
As quick as a wink, before we can blink
We feel a big change in our lives

The one whom we prayed for with tears in our eyes
The one whom we thought would stay lost
Is brought into sight by Heaven's good grace
Yes, at last our paths have crossed

And bright turns our lives as the day we now see
"Oh, God, there's such beauty in living"
We're so glad we're alive, we give thanks to God
For the beauty of life He is giving

TWO LONELY PEOPLE

Two lonely people sad and blue
Two lonely people with nothing to do
Two lonely people with no one to share
Two lonely people with no one to care

Two lonely people who cry at night
Hoping and praying for love's sweet sight
Two lonely people who want joy, too
Like two other people who found their love true

Two lonely people hoping their feet
Will take them somewhere where they'll meet
Two lonely people with arms opened wide
Hoping for someone to come inside

Two lonely people in a world so big
Looking in the forest for a twig
Two lonely people praying hard and true
That you'll find me and I'll find you

MY SAVIOUR AND YOU

I turned my head and I looked all around
My eyes swallowed all they could see
Such a beautiful feeling, one I couldn't explain
All at once was now part of me

I raised my glance to the Heavens on high
The smile from my heart was astounding
How wondrous the glory which now filled my soul
Every part of my being was pounding

I winked at the sun; I smiled with the moon
I danced with the stars in the sky
I straddled the rainbow; I rolled on the clouds
I sang with the angels on high

Life is so beautiful for now I'm alive
A new start has been given to me
I'm born once again; I am totally new
All the beauty of life I now see

What is the reason for this joy I now feel
Why is there song in my heart
Why do I thank my good Lord above
Why does now, my life, finally start

The answer is, oh, so very clear
All the bad in my life reached an end
My Saviour had shown He truly loves me
When He gave me you as a friend

REMEMBER TO FORGET

I try to remember to try to forget
The good in my life I lost and yet
Forgetting is hard when remembering you
I can't forget how I loved you so true

I remember the times when you were mine
I can't forget the flowers and wine
And the happiness when remembering you
Promised you'd never forget me, too

I try to remember to try to forget
But I forget to remember I can't forget
Some day the memories will fade away
And I'll forget to remember the happy day

And now as I sit and remember you
I wonder if you remember me, too
Those beautiful days are gone and yet
I still can't remember to forget

HOW DO YOU KNOW?

The look, the sigh, the gleam in the eye
Are more beauty of life than stars in the sky
The words of endearment; the gentle caress
Are the total, supreme sense of pure happiness

The sweet little nothings whispered in your ear
Are the most important words you will ever hear
The little touch of a hand on your face
From love is more powerful than a total embrace

A sincere little smile meant only for you
Is more than a world full of laughter you knew
The quick, fleeting touch as your loved one walks by
Has more charge than the lightning which comes from the sky

Your loved one beside you when things go wrong
Makes you feel all is right and once more you are strong
When you're with your loved one, wherever it be
There's no other person you'd care to see

A telephone call, anytime, night or day
Especially when there's nothing to say
Is as being near the one you love so
It keeps you together and says more than you know

These are the acts of a love deep and true
They're the ways of knowing your loved one loves you
They can't be restrained, to be shown how they thrive
And as long as they are there, you know love is alive

ASK HIM, PLEASE

Kneel down softly
Close your eyes
Say a prayer or two
Speak to God in Heaven above
Speak for me and for you

Ask him of the promises
The things, He said, would be
Ask Him of the beauty
You and I would see

Ask Him of the miracles
The impossible He would do
Ask Him of the blessings
For those who love Him true

For those who obeyed his every word
Ask of their reward
For those who followed His Heavenly laws
Ask of the happiness they implored

Ask Him of the love
Ask Him of the peace
Ask Him of the hatred
Which seems to, never, cease

Ask Him of the forgiveness
Of our ignorant behavior
Ask Him of the words from the Cross
Which came from our dying Saviour

Please, ask our Lord in Heaven
Of the good He promised would be
He'll tell you all He said was true
If you open your heart and see

I DON'T WISH WHAT I WISH

If there were three wishes granted to me
This is exactly what they would be:

The first two I'd wish
For the Third to come true
The third would be
You would say, "I love you"

If the lamp of Aladdin were mine to be found
And the Genie brought power to me
I would give him his freedom instead of command
If your love were mine to see

If the Gypsy told me
Spin around, count to three
All the riches of life I would share

I'd not count past two
If I knew there was you
I'd have wealth if, for me
You would care

No Genie, no Gypsy, no wishes there'd be
If only you'd say -
You love me

OUR MAKER

With one wave of His hand He made the Sun
A flick of His finger and the Moon was done
From the sparkling glow within his eyes
He gave a wink, there were Star filled skies

A move of His head, the clouds were there
A pull of His breath and there was air
The sweat from His brow, with one quick shake
Brought forth the raindrop; the pure snowflake

"Give warmth my creations", the Sun was told
"Bring beauty of night", to the Moon He spoke bold
"For my children on earth you will have light
You'll hear all their wishes, Star light, Star bright"

His children He made with special care
A handful of dust and man was there
He plucked from the chest of this one who lie bare
One rib - made it woman - for his love to share

He spoke and He said, "I made you from love
Look all around you, look up above
Study them well, these sights you now see
They're yours for one reason, to remind you of me"

"More beauty awaits you if this life you live well
But awaken my wrath and you shall know hell
You, man, are the husband; woman, you are his wife
Now go walk the earth and bring forth more life"

"Pass on all my wishes to those you do make
For once I'm forgotten this earth I'll forsake
I give you the choice; free will now is yours
To obey all my wishes; my wishes are laws"

These actions occurred a long time ago
How many of us, today, do God know
Is He happy or sad, has man lived life wise
Look well around you, what see *your* eyes

THE OFFICE PRAYER

It's the end of the week; the time for fun
Thank God it's Friday; this week's work is done
Five days of labor; the same old routine
For two happy days now, here I won't be seen

My boss with that grouchy look on his face
Won't see me till Monday in this lousy place
My life is my own; no rules to obey
Come and go as I want to; I'll make my own day

Out dining and dancing; a movie I'll see
Stay up at night and watch some T.V.
For two solid days I won't look at that clock
It can hang on that wall, to itself can tick tock

The strings on this puppet of labor I cut
I've got two days to get myself out of this rut
No pencils, no pens, no business phone calls
I won't feel till Monday these closing four walls

No Mister, Miss, Mrs, or Ms, as may be
I'll mingle with people with first names, like me
Oh, Friday night, Saturday and Sunday, too
You beautiful weekend, how I love you

MY ONE, ONLY WISH

If the world were mine to have and to hold
And the riches of life were mine, too
I'd give them all up; I'd give them away
If my one, only, wish would come true

If they made me a King, the world to command
And the universe I controlled, too
I'd step down from my throne, cast my crown to the stone
If my one, only, wish would come true

I don't want power
I don't want lust
I'd give my life
Return to dust

I'd crawl on my hands
Serve the whole world, too
If my one, only, wish would come true

Nothing there is I'd want to own
For there's nothing I'd rather have, than
My one, my only, wish in life -

- to live with my children again

LOVE'S HOPE

"I love you!"

This sensation within my soul is so deep, so strong, so pure.
My heart cannot understand why this thunderous power is
not felt by you. Perhaps it is felt but cast off as flakes of snow
resting atop your shoulders on a cold, wintry, night. I seek,
only, perfection for your soul; the fulfillment of your mind.
I yearn to be, to you, what the sun is to summer; the frost to
winter. I seek to be the ultimate satisfaction for your body.

"I love you!"

Yet, my love goes unused. This love of mine must have an outlet
for it is as the waters pressing against the dam. Each time you come
into sight more drops of love fill me, yet, still remain stored.

***Is love, not permitted freedom, wasted, as is the fruit of the tree
untouched by human hands?***

The sun bathes the earth with light and warmth yet rests at night.
The snows cover the ground in a blanket of pure white, yet, soon
melt away. This love of mine cannot sleep, cannot melt. It is the
wish of my God that no love should go unused. Am I, then, to
bathe another in this river of affection which, endlessly, flows
within me? Would this be then fair to the laws of pure love?

But this love of mine must be used. It must be set free. I must
relieve this constant pressure which fills my heart. It would go to
another as a false love. The true taste of the juice of my love would
be somewhat bittered if not poured into the one my life seeks - you!

I do not know how long I can wait. How long can a cloud keep the rain in its bosom before it bursts? Am I destined to live in uncertainty, ever wondering if you would have opened your heart to mine? No matter how long the wait, would I have acted in haste? Or should I fight this urge to set free this storm of love which brews within me and, perhaps, carry it with me into the endless day of eternity?

I leave this decision to you, my love, and to my maker.

I will kneel in prayer, ever waiting, for one sign of hope I shall not err in my life. I sit in prayer and beg the Queen of Peace to whisper into your ear; to awaken you to the beauty; I alone can give to you.

I wait for you, my love, until . . .

THE SEASONS OF LIFE

Oh, pretty flower standing tall
Where do you go when comes the fall
And grass, and leaves, and all that's green
The end of the summer, to you, seems mean

Pretty birds which fly the sky so blue
When the chill arrives I won't see you
No bathing, no beaches, no fun in the sand
Old man winter brings barren land

No more walks at night by the moon
Yes, the summer seems to end too soon
In place of the warmth, the romantic air
Will be frost and icicles, here and there

There won't be much for me to do
Summer, oh Summer, how I'll miss you
Nothing to do when there is snow
With the freezing air, where can I go?

Out come the coats, the scarves, the gloves
The too short days with no sun above
I'll have to be content with the white, white, snow
The snowmen, the sleigh rides, balls of snow to throw

The fun and the frolic in the blanket of white
Say, maybe fun will still fill the night
The cup of hot chocolate for you and for me
After we travel the mountain by ski

Ice skating on the lake in the park
Cuddling by the fireside after dark
Then there'll be the yuletide days
When peace and happiness guide our ways

Santa Clause, the Christmas tree
Good will toward men for you and for me
The parties, the fun, the songs to sing
The happy New Year, the hopes it'll bring

Yes, Mother Nature isn't bad at all
There's life to live, Summer, Winter, Spring and Fall

MY MOM

When my world was dark and filled with fear
Always so faithfully she'd be there
To comfort me when I needed it so
And she'd stay by my side till the fear would go

She sacrificed most of her life for me
Gave up her pleasures, the things she could be
I caused her pain but she didn't cry
Instead she gave thanks to God by that look in her eye

I took her for granted, never said thanks
For the pleasures she gave to me
For after all, wasn't it true
What would she be without me?

Yes, I placed no importance on her life
I never thought she had feelings, too
I made her grow old before her time
Yet for me, she'd find more to do

It's never until it's too late in life
That our eyes are opened wide
Too late to make life a little less hard
For that one who stood at our side

I wish I could go back in time, just once
Knowing everything that I now know
I'd make life a whole lot brighter for her
Just by saying, "Mom, *I love you so*"

MY GIFT FOR YOUR LOVE

I would capture a star from out of the sky
Wrap it up in a cloud of white
Tie it tight with a ray of sunshine
If you said you love me tonight

I would climb to the moon on my ladder of love
And paint on its face so bright
A picture of joy for the world to see
If you said you love me tonight

Who could hold back the reins of a love set free
Who could soften the strongest wind
Who could stop all the drops of happiness
That the clouds, with joys weep, begin

Who could harness the power of my true love
Who could push back the tide to the sea
Who could quiet applause of the thunder
If, tonight, you said you love me

LISTEN TO OUR FRIEND

There's a friend we have in common
Who knows how I love you
I told Him all my feelings
He knows my love is true

I beg and beg Him every day
To tell you how I feel
I hope soon He tells you
My feelings are so real

These words I cannot tell you
For you might believe them not
I'm so afraid they'll come out wrong
And keep us far apart

So when our friend does tell you
Of the things I wish to be
I know you will believe His words
And fall in love with me

I'll know the way you look at me
The way your head will nod
That He finally has spoken
And you heard the words of God

WHY DO I DREAM?

All of those happy days lived in the past
Those sweet, precious moments which never did last
The memories recalled from the depth of my mind
The laughter, the joy, the times no more to find

Why do I dream?

Those beautiful days when I walked in the sun
Those happy filled days when life just begun
The places, the faces, of the loved ones so true
The long ago, far away, times that I knew

Why do I dream?

The smiles which were given only to me
The look in my loved ones eyes that I would see
The words, the movements from those I knew love
The treasures God sent me from Heaven above

Why do I dream?

The beautiful times in my life are gone yet
They visit me nightly so I can't forget
Maybe they're saying love fades not away
The Blessings from God forever do stay

Is that why I dream?????

OUR LIVES OF NIGHT

The golden hue of day slowly dims leaving way for
the dark shadow of night

Night

The essence of time which permits the pent up memories
within our minds to, once again, enjoy the sweet
taste of freedom

The memories are free to dance amidst the blanket
of cover which comes with the night

There is no need, now, to close our eyes

Gaze into the darkened chasm of the sky and see
all the beauty which lie asleep in our minds
during the bright of day

Listen to the past speaking out amidst the darkened
quiescence of night

The world sleeps
The beauties of nature rest

Our tired bodies slow to the unhastened pace they
assume during the peaceful tranquility of night

There is no need, now, to beckon to our memories

The night offers a continuous invitation to come
forth - to come, again, alive as in the miracle of re-incarnation

It is the memories recalled from the background
of our mind which lullaby us into the synonym of death - sleep

Even in this valley of rest - sleep - our memories
prance about in our vision whispering to us it
is now that our past and present become united
- Share the same movements of time

And as the night moves, slowly, past the brim of
the horizon, we awaken to another light filled day

Awaken to feed into the memory of our mind more beauty
-Beauty which will again live in the future -
or the present - of the night -

The night to be

JUST KNOWING YOU

Whenever I look at the stars in the skies
I see, in my mind, your sparkling eyes
When I stare at the Moon my heart starts to race
For the Moon casts a glow of your beautiful face

When the Sun shines brightly for my eyes to see
I feel, deep within, the warmth you give me
As the gay, carefree cloud rolls joyfully by
It's your charm, your grace I see with my eye

It's your soft tender touch I feel by the hour
As I hold in my hand a beautiful flower
As the wind makes the tree and the grass dance with glee
It's the beauty of living you bring unto me

The feeling of newness you bring makes me sigh
As the feeling of hearing a baby's first cry
It's you, only you, who makes living worthwhile
When your eyes look at mine and you give me your smile

It's just knowing you that makes my life shine
And I wish, how I wish—

You were all mine

THEN YOU'RE IN LOVE WITH ME

If I make you happy
Being who you are
If you feel peace within you
Whether near me or afar
If I can make you smile
When you gaze upon a star

Then you're in love with me

If there's no other place
You'd rather be
When, my darling, you're beside me

If when, my sweetheart,
You're looking at me
There's no other person
You'd care to see

Then you're in love with me

If, because of me, the Sun shines bright
And you're never lonely when alone at night
If the world to you is a beautiful sight

Then you're in love with me

More

APPRECIATE YOUR WIFE

Remember when you were all alone
There was one thing you thought, always, of
You dreamed so hard; you wished and prayed
For the day when you'd find love

Remember how your prayer was answered
When she first came into your life
From the very first moment you saw her
You knew she'd be your wife

You showered her with attention
She was constantly on your mind
You took her everywhere with you
You treated her so kind

Whatever it was she desired
How gladly you filled her need
No one could ever accuse you
Of thoughtlessness or greed

And so in love she married you
For you were the joy in her heart
She vowed to God in Heaven
From you she'd never part

She cleaned your house; she washed your clothes
She cooked your food every day
She made you feel like a man in the world
She catered to your every way

Now it's time for you to look deep in her eyes
Do you still see joy in her soul
Does the look which comes from deep within
Show she still has the same loving goal

Go to your woman and hug her tightly
Let her know she's all in your life
Kiss her, caress her, whisper in her ear

"I appreciate my wife"

MY GIFT OF LOVE TO YOU

I can't give you the Sun; can't buy you the Moon
Can't bring you the Stars or an angel's tune
The clouds are not mine to lay at your feet
I own, not the rain, the snow or the sleet

I have even nothing on this big earth
To give you, my love, that has some worth
I'm a pauper, a peasant, a ragged man, too
But my gesture of love is this song for you

My song is the wealth I find in your face
My tune is the riches I'll ever embrace
Each note is a beat of my heart so true
Together they are my love song to you

If my song you would sing
I'd no longer be poor
For the music I'd hear
Would open the door
To all that the world
Could bestow upon me
My love song to you
Sung by you -

-Sung to me

WHY ME?

I am but a mortal, a man sometimes weak
Then the will of my God, the reason I seek
I know deep in my soul God loves us as one
Yet I can't understand why some things are done

I know I must suffer so strong I may be
But in times of my weakness I say, "God, why me?"
I know pain I must feel so more I can bear
Yet sometimes I ask, "God, are you still here?"

I know darkness must enter my life as the night
So true beauty I'll know when God shines the light
I know my eyes must, at times, shed a tear
So the sadness that awaits me, my life will then bear

I know no one in life ever lives without pain
Not one living person ever sees not the rain
I know everyone shares the hardships of life
We all have our times of nothing but strife

I know I stand not alone in times of life's grief
And more times than others I accept my belief
So I ask true forgiveness when I fail so to see
God give me the strength to ask not -

Why me?

MY GARDEN OF LOVE

I planted a flower
I planted a tree
The seeds of grass
I spread carefully
I showered the earth
With misty dew
To grow a garden of love for you

For you were the flower of my life
You were my grass so green
You were the garden of life to me
With more beauty than I've ever seen

I tend to the flower, the grass and the tree
I care for them ever so true
For this is my garden, my garden of love
I grew, my darling, for you

MY LITTLE CHILD'S SMILE

What could take the sadness from my face
What could bring the joy back in its place
What could make life bright
Fill me with Sunlight

- My little child's smile -

What could make a mountain a very small hill
What could make the forest invisible
What could calm the sea
Bring peace to me

- My little child's smile -

And when the world is dark
No Sun above
What could make me know
I still have love

When I walk a path
That seems unpure
What could set me straight
Make my steps sure

What is God's love from up above—

—My little child's smile—

OUR LOVE

How beautiful the love the two of us share
Our love for each other will, ever, be there
We don't love each other the way others do
Our love is different, each day it starts new

Whenever you see me you give me a smile
The love in your face makes living worthwhile
The beautiful glow from within your eyes
Shows me our love is as tall as the skies

When around other people, of me, you still think
You catch my eye and you give me a wink
You throw me a kiss when no one can see
You pucker your lips and blow softly towards me

On the beach we walk, always, hand in hand
You run and I chase you in the sand
I pick you up and I spin you around
We laugh very hard as we fall to the ground

The laughing stops, your eyes fix in a stare
As I kiss your face gently and I stroke your hair
The look of love comes over your face
As I hold you tightly in love's sweet embrace

I hug you and I kiss you; I squeeze you so tight
Your lips press to mine so strong yet so light
We lie on the sand, my arms around you
I say I love you, you say you love me, too

We were bless'd, my darling, by the Lord on high
And our love will grow stronger even after we die
Then even in Heaven, for all time to be
Together with God, it'll be just you and me

BE THANKFUL FOR
WHAT YOU HAVE

One day my son was very sad
He wasn't happy with what he had
He felt, in life, he was very poor
He wanted to know why he couldn't have more
I picked him up and sat him on my knee
And told him a story that was once told to me:

My son, I said, when I'm sad and blue
And the world seems full of harm
I think of this man whom I once knew
This man had only one arm

The man with one arm had less than me
And that made me feel so fine
But don't worry about him, I was told
For it's that way down the line

The man with one arm at times was glum
Till he met a man and this man had none
The man with no arms, for pity, didn't beg
For he knew someone with no arms and one leg

The man with no arms and one leg there
Met another with no arms and no legs to spare
The man with no limbs was not filled with despair
For he knew one with no limbs and who also couldn't hear
The man with no limbs and ears not alright
Knew someone like him but who had, also, no sight

On and on the story could go
For someone with less than you, you'll always know
So don't live your life always looking for more
You have much more than others, my son, that's for sure

THE NIGHT STRANGER

The other night while sleeping tight
I heard a noise inside
It woke me up - It got me scared
It made me want to hide

I stepped down from my nice warm bed
And I tip-toed to the door
I opened it so quietly
Then I heard a sound once more

My eyes searched all around the room
The light was very dim
I saw a person moving
I was really scared of him

I wanted to call mom and dad
For them to come and help me
But I could only stand there
Shaking nervously

He walked around, looked here and there
What was he looking for
I hoped he wouldn't notice me
Peeking through the door

I swallowed hard, took a deep breath
I knew it was all up to me
I'd have to try and fight him off
And protect my family

I flung the door, it opened wide
I quickly jumped and ran inside
I found the light and turned it on
So that he couldn't hide

He must've heard me coming
Because he disappeared
He wasn't where he could be found
I guess I really got him scared

I searched the room so thoroughly
To see just what he took
There was nothing missing
I guess I really foiled that crook

I looked outside the window
To make sure he was gone
Then I heard the doorbell ring
I called my dad and mom

Mom came inside and she opened the door
She wasn't scared because
She had to let my dad back in

Oops! I mean Santa Clause

THE SENIOR CITIZEN

Who laid the groundwork for you and for me
Who made the things, today, we see
Who worked long hours every day
Who are the ones who led the way

The Senior Citizen.

Who worked and built with plain, bare, hands
No fancy machines to take commands
Whose sweat is part of the whole country
Who broke his back for you and for me

The Senior Citizen.

Who cooked the food straight from the land
Never saw food come already canned
Who cooked with coal, used an icebox
No instant dinner, no food in a box

The Senior Citizen.

Who used to live by candlelight
Never had time to relax at night
Who listened to stories on the radio
Never knew the meaning of a T.V. show

The Senior Citizen.

Who are the ones with heads held high
Who will live with pride till the day they die
Who are the ones who deserve a rest
Our Senior Citizen with whom we were blessed

I'M A HARDENED CRIMINAL

I've committed a crime; I've been unjust
I'm a menace to society and pay I must
I'm a hardened criminal, the cops caught me
And soon, very soon, convicted I'll be

No, I didn't murder; I didn't steal
The crime I committed was dangerous, unreal
I didn't push drugs; Rape isn't my line
If these were my crimes I'd get off just fine

I didn't mug; A kidnaper I'm not
I don't explode bombs; I don't smoke pot
These crimes are plain, they're not for me
Heck, a slap on the wrist and free I'd be

My crime is the worst ever heard by far -
Today I illegally parked my car

THE MOST FEARED MAN
IN THE WORLD

He doesn't look tough, even mean enough
Yet he makes us shiver with fear
Whenever we see him we want to run
We wish he wasn't near

He acts as though he hasn't a care
He knows we cower when he is there
He's nobody's idol, his friends are few
One glance from him and you know you're through

Even children hide when they see him come
They shake, and they cry, and they throw a tantrum
Women don't come and flock at his feet
For even to women he's not very sweet

The biggest of men tried to call his bluff
But he just stands there, they know he's tough
They turn around and they run like hell
They haven't a chance and they know it well

But again and again, we stand up to him
We try to show we're strong within
We look him up and we clench our fist
As we sit in the chair of our dentist

THE STAR WITH A TEAR

There's a little star with a tear in its eye
"Why, little star, do you cry in the sky?"
The Little Star, so sad and blue
Said, "Cause I cannot twinkle for people like you"

"I try and I try but my light is steady
The other stars go on and off when they're ready
I can't give beauty to people in love
They don't look at me when they look up above"

I said to the star, "You cry in vain
You're a special star, you aren't plain
The night will come and very soon
You'll be good luck for all the lovers in June"

"You can't twinkle, you're a very rare star
People will see you and know what you are
You'll give people hope whether near or afar
You're the reason for wishing—

—*You're a shooting star*"

THE BRIGHT HAPPY DAY

In my mind I remember the bright, happy day
The long time ago, long ago, far away
The time in my life there were clouds at my feet
And the true taste of life was so bland and so sweet

With the tip of my finger I toyed with the Sun
The top of the rainbow was my seat, shared by none
To the Moon I would smile as it rolled past my eye
As the Stars formed a halo circling me in the sky

The world was my toy that I played with at will
Atop the tallest of mountains I was king of the hill
The vast, endless, desert was my box filled with sand
The deep winding river I swirled with my hand

In my mind I remember the bright, happy day
But they're gone, yes, they're gone—

—*Oh, so far away*

THE POEM OF LOVE FROM YOU

The words from the Bible I saved for another day
The books of philosophers I put away
The sayings of the prophets are locked away, too
I only want to read these words from you

Your love is a poem on one page
A page I will cherish through my old age
You gave me your heart with words that rhyme
These words will fill my soul till the end of time

The words of all the poets don't interest me
The writings of our fathers mean nothing to me
The laws of life, on paper, I won't read, too
My eyes can only see these words from you

You wrote me a poem of your true love
The words from your pen came from Heaven above
Your hand was guided by the Lord on high
I'll recite your poem till the day I die

The ABC's of life, I'll read them not
Stories by famous authors, I forgot
Letters in the mail are unopened, too
The only thing I read is the poem of love from you

ONLY THROUGH GOD

Acquaintances I have, thousands of
I know people all around the earth
But I'm thankful to God in Heaven above
For giving me friends above my worth

There are people in my life very close to me
I'll call them my friends my life through
For no matter what I am, or ever will be
They stay by my side ever true

There were days when my life was so very low
I thought, never, would I rise again
In those times of my need my friends didn't go
They stayed close to me, even then

When I got back up on my own two feet
I never bothered once to give thanks
But still they stayed, didn't run in retreat
Never even wavered to the flanks

As long as I live, until my life ends
I'll smile, happily, to Heaven above
For only through God does a man get friends
Friends who give you all their love

OF LIFE AND LOVE

"I am loved"

Is there anything in the world, made or done by man, that will ever bear more fruit than this simple phrase? Since the beginning of time these words have been taught by God. This is all He has ever asked us to live, to show - love. Is it not true a man without love is as the ocean without water? As the sky without the Sun, Stars, or Moon? It is the blessing God delivered by His hand which makes a man know love. To be loved is to be of God. To be loved is to know the Heavenly way. From birth we are taught to love God. Love, then, is the true weapon of the universe. Love received is more victorious than all the wars ever won. Love received is greater than any other aspiration desired by man.

If I am loved does it not mean I share the wish of God? Though no love could ever be as tall as the love given to God, is it not just as beautiful to know one tree in the forest is mine?

If I am loved it means I am free of evil for no one loves evil. I am not a saint, though. I am a mortal man and perfection is, to me, unattainable. I, however, must bear more good than bad, if I am loved.

To be loved is to be deserving of love. To be deserving of love I must be, constantly, attuned to the needs of the one from whom I receive love. I might, at times, falter in my awareness of the needs of this love, however, if I tend to the seed of this love, the tree of the seed will be strong enough to overcome the pain of one leaf plucked from its branch.

I must try, always, to be deserving of love. I must maintain in my mind that love, if not caressed, will, as any other product of nature, wither and eventually die. It is known love is a part of life. Is it realized life is a drama? In my drama, the drama of life, to be loved is the greatest gift of all. I, however, seek another gift: The gift of appreciation.

I will try to be as appreciative of your love as is humanly possible. I will accept you for what and for whom you are. I will overcome your alien moods knowing you, too, are not of pure perfection but, also, bear the flaws of man.

I will, however, remember the perfections you *do* possess and I will put them first in my mind during those times of your weakness. I will, at times, be glad you falter in your ways so I may prove to be the pillar on which you may lean. My faith to you will be taller than the mountain which kisses the sky!

I need your love
I am proud of your love
I am strong with your love

When I find myself at the mercy of the lions in the den of life, brutally beaten, subject to despair, your lips speaking, "I love you", and my heart knowing and feeling your words will awaken in me the strength to fight, the strength I knew not existed in me. I will defeat the enemy seen, as well as unseen. I will climb from the shadow of defeat. Yes, I will emerge from the pit of calamity in answer to your call of love.

"I am loved"

Science has not yet invented a medicine as powerful as the healing power of these words. Man has not yet assembled an army large enough to equal the strength of this phrase. The devil will never create a temptation powerful enough to turn my head so I might not hear these beautiful words you utter.

"I am loved"

The most rewarding embrace of life. My eyes will ever see your lips speak these words. My sense of sound will fondle, endlessly, these words I hear. These words, your actions, will instill in me the full glow of the blessing of God throughout eternity.

"I am loved"

"You, too, are loved"

MY LITTLE GIRL

I waited and waited; I paced to and fro
The clock on the wall seemed not to go
It felt there I spent my whole life through
Counting the seconds waiting for you

After what seemed an eternity
A nurse called my name and quietly
I walked toward you, my mind in a whirl
I took my first glimpse of my little girl

You were wrapped in a blanket, in a glass case
My eyes became misty when I saw your face
My heart and my soul filled quickly with love
For my beautiful present from God above

I cherished those moments there by your side
My body was shaking as it filled with pride
My lips tried to utter a word or two
But the lump in my throat wouldn't let my speech through

So I spoke to you, sweetheart, I spoke from the heart
My heart started shouting as the nurse made us part

No song could be sung; no words put into rhyme
Man will never find ways till the end of all time
To describe the feeling, the feeling divine
Of when father sees daughter for the very first time

Words can't tell the feeling receiving God's charms
When taking you home you were placed in my arms
I carried you as though I were walking on eggs
All the strength in my body I sent to my legs

Then into our home, through our front door
I carried you, my daughter, in my arms once more
Watching you grow, day by day
Brought joy to my life in every way

When I fed you your bottle in the middle of the night
I'll remember, till I die, that wonderful sight
Your big, beautiful, eyes staring at mine
No feeling on earth could be more sublime

Days turned to weeks, weeks to months rolled by
I remember your laughter, the times you did cry
The restless nights, the fears you felt
The times you were sick, by your bed how I knelt

You crawled every room, you were here, you were there
How you laughed when I found you hiding under a chair
And how proud I was that day I did see
You took your first step, your first step to me

I hugged you so tightly, such joy you did bring
Watching you grow up made my heart sing
And after my days work when I reached home once more
How you ran into my arms as I walked in the door

The problems, the worries, from my job that grew
All at once disappeared as I held you
Each night after dinner on the floor we stayed
For hours and hours, together, we played

Then I sat on the couch to watch some T.V.
You sat on my lap with your arms around me
You sat there so still, you made not a peep
For during the movie you fell off to sleep

I carried you lightly; carried you to your bed
Tucked you in, sat a while; then kissed your forehead
As I reached the door, I went to turn off the light
I stared at you, darling, then whispered good night

I took only two steps, maybe three
When I heard your sweet voice calling, "Daddy"
I flicked on the switch, the room filled with light
My heart melted quickly at your beautiful sight.

Your eyes opened wide were all I could see
I knew they were saying, "Please stay here with me"
I sat on your bed, we quietly spoke
How you laughed every time I told you a joke

Then the words stopped, your eyes fixed in a stare
As I tickled you softly and I stroked your hair
Another memory for me to keep
You had to be tickled or you couldn't sleep

It was something I really wanted to do
For it gave me more reason to just look at you
In a matter of minutes you were fast asleep
I kissed you and kissed you; our love was so deep

The years rolled by quickly, so quickly they flew
I remember the night I stayed up with you
You were so scared, my darling, you cried a big pool
For tomorrow would be your first day of school

Your birthdays, your school days, how quickly they passed
Your sick days, your glad days, they went by too fast
Your homework, your projects, all that you made
Your test marks, report cards, grade after grade

We did so much together who thought there would be
That day in our lives you'd be taken from me
One day there was joy, happiness in the air
The next day your room was empty and bare

Now that you're gone and there's nothing but space
I still look and see your beautiful face
We had nine years together, you and me
Now all I have is your memory

Gone are the dresses, the ribbons and bows
Gone is your laughter, your cute little nose
Yes, my little girl's gone, you were taken from me
You sit now, my sweetheart, on a new Daddy's knee

Your memories are here, they're burned in my mind
And I pray to God one day I'll find
Your sweet, smiling, face will be there once more
When I come home from work and I open the door

Without you, my sweetheart, my life is so bare
I go back in time to the days you were here
The pain in my heart, each day, starts anew
My life has no meaning now, none without you

Please God in Heaven, please hear my prayer
Please bring back my daughter, please let her be here

From this moment on, my precious one
Only in dreams I see things left undone
I sit in my chair and I stare at the wall
And I pretend we're together sharing our all

It would've been great, though it makes me feel sad
As I picture you saying, "Can I talk to you, Dad"
Then seeing you blush, finding words hard to speak
"Dad, a boy in my class wants to date me next week"

Yes, one joy in life I'll never see
Your very first date and how nervous you'd be
Trying to find the right dress to wear
Making sure no one messes your hair

Seeing you shake as you answer the door
Trying to show him you did it before
And the look on your face so happy and glad
As you say to your fellow, "This is my Dad"

And then one day when you're sure I'm ready
I'd hear you say you want to go steady
And the times to follow when you and me
Would talk of the problems of love you would see

Then for hours and hours on the phone you'd be
Gosh, you'd never have time anymore for me
As a matter of fact you'd never see me there
I'd just be that man, the old timer, the square

A few years later you'd make my heart sing
As you tell me you're getting an engagement ring
I'd hold you and I'd hug you, so proud I'd be
Then I'd go to the bathroom so my tears you won't see

Then the big day when side by side
I'd walk down the aisle with my daughter, a bride
Yes, I'd lose you, my little girl, you'd go away
But at least I'd know you'd come back some day

Back with your husband to see your old Dad
I'd get kind of misty, yet happy, not sad
For I know I would play on the floor once more
Sit on the bed, tickle and talk as before
Yes, life would be happy, so happy I'd be
To start life anew - my granddaughter and me

God bless you, my little girl.; God bless you
Your Daddy loves you for eternity through

Good night, my sweetheart, wherever you are!

I love you!

WYMMIKITOFY

AT LONG LAST HE SPEAKS

All my life I've prayed to God
With basically one request
I've asked Him over and over again
How will I know when I'm bless'd

And then one day:

The Sun shone through and spoke to me
The Moon and the Stars shared words, too
The rainbow arched over my head
And whispered God's words so true

The Mountain stood tall and called my name
As the Trees swayed and told me God's story
The River, the Lake, the little old Pond
All shared with me God's words of glory

All of God's creatures turned to me
In unison they uttered God's word
The melody I heard from atop my shoulder
Was sung by a beautiful bird

Then the clouds parted; the sky opened wide
I saw God's Face shining through
He touched my head as He answered my prayer
He said, "I sent your true love to you"

OUR FINAL DESTINY

Destiny - the end of the road
Our fate in life, our final abode
The path to the end is different for all
But the end is the same be the path large or small

Our road is our choice, our guide is our mind
Though we try to foresee what our journey will find
We weigh with our caution which road we shall take
But how is one told the right choice he did make

We ponder this question our entire life through
Never knowing, ever hoping, our decision was true
We share our adventures with the ones we hold dear
And make our true judgment based on hardships we hear

And yet when we pause in the walk of our life
We gaze back and recall the weight of our strife
Those burdens, disappointments, which we met in our day
How compare they with those had we gone a different way

Only God up above our life can foresee
And the truly wise man prays for guidance daily
He accepts what is met, and he bears no regret
For the kingdom of Heaven is awaiting us yet

MY DAY IN CHURCH

I went to Church to say a prayer
For I was lonely, filled with despair
I walked down the aisle, my steps I could hear
The Church was deserted, so empty, so bare

I sat myself down in the nearest pew
The Church seemed enormous as empty things do
There wasn't a sound, the lights were so dim
My eyes roamed around then settled on Him

He was nailed to a cross with His arms opened wide
His head hung in sorrow, blood from His heart cried
As I sat and I watched Him, I felt sorrow so deep
As I thought of His life my eyes started to weep

My worries and problems seemed so small to me
Compared to His burdens, the life He did see
My eyes studied, carefully, the saints by His side
The look in His mother's eyes, for they watched as He died

Such pain, such sorrow, they all must have felt
I slipped from my seat and in deep prayer I knelt
I found myself asking forgiveness of Him
For 'twas people as me who made His life dim

How could I compare my grievance with this
A family of sorrow who, on earth, never knew bliss
I sat and I sat and I stared and I stared
All at once my heart pounded, I got so scared

I couldn't believe it, how could it be
All the saints in the Church turned and looked at me
The Lord raised His head as He faced my way
I thought to myself, "This is my last day"

The lights in the Church all at once seemed so bright
Brighter and brighter like rays of sunlight
The silence was broken as the Church bells rang
There was beautiful music as angels sang

All the saints in the Church faced him and knelt
I must be in Heaven for that's how it felt
He stepped from His cross, angels sang in glee
Yet strangely enough He stared straight at me

He opened His arms, His face wore a smile
He said to me, softly, "Come here, my child"
I lifted my body from out of its seat
And as though as on air I was placed at His feet

I lie on the floor before God, my King
And louder and louder the angels did sing
Though I closed my eyes still I could see
The bright lights all around and Him before me

He spoke to me softly as He touched my head
Every word was like music, every word He said
When He was through He asked one thing of me
He asked me to honor His Mother, Mary

I turned my head, slightly, so her I could see
Truly she was full of grace and beauty
Slowly she started to fade from my view
My heart cried out loudly, "Please take me with you"

She raised her hand in a gesture of love
Her smile told me clearly, "In Heaven above
Someday, my child, our home you will share
If your love for the Lord and for me is there"

I promised and promised, "Forever there'd be
Nothing but love in my heart for thee"
When they were gone, away from my sight
The angels stopped singing; away went the light

I closed my eyes; I felt no worry or fear
I was at peace with myself, I knew God was here
I have no recall rising to my feet
But when I opened my eyes, I was back in my seat

Everything was as it had been before
Except me, I felt different, I had faith once more
For the rest of my life I'll never be sure
If I had a dream - had a dream or . . . ??????

THE POWER OF YOUR LOVE

While walking the night sad and blue
My feet led me straight there to you
I stopped and I stared; asked myself if you cared
Then I left thinking we two were through

A tear from my eye I did shed
So I stopped and I turned back my head
My heart started to race as I pictured your face
By some power toward you I was led

Slowly I climbed the stairs to your floor
Wondering if I could see you once more
I knew not if you cared; knew not if I dared
Have the courage to open your door

I reached out; my hand trembling so
I felt I quickly should go
I knew why I was blue; I was unfair to you
My true love I never did show

The door opened with one little shove
I could feel all the glory of love
I'm here in your grace, my heart found its place
Back in your Church, my sweet Lord above

ALTHOUGH

I love you, my darling

I've loved you since the beginning of time

I've loved you every moment of every hour of every day

I've loved the feeling which swirled through my entire
being every time I saw your beautiful face

I've loved the glow of love which sparkled from deep
within your eyes

I've loved the soft smoothness of your tender skin touching mine

I've loved the warmth of your comforting smile

I've loved the sweet, tender, melody of your angelical voice

I've loved the deep mystery of you

My darling:

I've loved the gentle touch of your hand on mine

I've loved the fragrance of your hair as you lay
your beautiful head on my shoulder

I've loved the feeling of love we experienced
as we gazed into each other's eyes

I've loved the love which erupted from the depth of our souls

I've loved the way the world shook whenever we'd
lie together in our sweet, ecstatic, moments of love

My darling:

I've loved you more than life itself

—You alone have given me reason to love
—You alone have given me reason to live

My darling, if ever anyone could count all the stars in the sky;
—And count every pebble on every path;
Every blade of grass in every meadow;
Every leaf on every tree:

If ever there were a way to count every drop of water
in every river, lake and pond:

Then, and only then, my sweet love

Would you know how much I love you

My darling, until time is no more - I will love you

- I have loved you -

- I do love you -

- I will love you, my precious one

Although -

- *We've never met!*

ANGEL OF RECORDS

There's an angel above in a large book filled space
He's the keeper of records for the whole human race
His job is not easy; he works nights and days
He plots all our courses; he charts all our ways

From the time we are born to the day stops our age
We follow the road he marks on each page
He knows where we'll go; the things we will do
Every minute's accounted for me and for you

Times few of us feel he does not his job well
Our path seems unwritten; we think we're in hell
For why should it be some live without pain
While others feel useless like lives lived in vain

We pray God in Heaven this angel send aid
An error in writing we think he has made
We feel that somewhere in our book up above
Should be much more written of joy, peace, and love

True, maybe that chapter is not yet embossed
But can it be that our book has been lost
Too many of us grow weary with age
Our lives spent in doubt if there is such a page

But if it is planned good things yet to be
Please, angel of records, write that page for me

MY FRIEND

A long time ago I walked in despair
Not one in the world I thought could care
I was lonely and lost; confused in my mind
It seemed all life had left me behind

But then one day for my eyes to see
Came into my life a friend true to me
She was so full of beauty both inside and out
I'm thankful I found her while wandering about

I spoke to her endlessly, crying my blue
She stood there and listened, her patience so true
The hours rolled by and she seemed not to mind
I never knew anyone could be so kind

She took in my troubles, shared none of her own
For once in my life I felt not alone
Then when it came time for me to depart
I could feel the good-bye came from her heart

I knew then and there she'd always be
Waiting whenever her I cared to see
I never gave thought to the rudeness I showed
For I never asked of the burdens she towed

I used her only for my selfish need
Yet she never reacted with anger or greed
When my spirits were high and I sought my own fun
I completely ignored her for her job was done

Yet when upon me came more empty space
I sought her and found her; a smile on her face
Although I was selfish; my good times unshared
Always it seemed she was there and she cared

What a wonderful world it surely would be
If all were like my friend -

-The Blessed Mary

THE WALK OF LIFE

I've lived many years on this big earth
It's been a long, long time since the day of my birth
And all through the years in this life that I've led
I've tried very hard to face straight ahead

I've learned the true meaning of happy and sad
Life taught me about the good and the bad
I knew the feeling of being on top
I've seen the bottom to which I did drop

There were times when I thought I knew what life was about
But experience taught me the meaning of doubt
In youth who cares how the dice are tossed
Now I've learned to be careful for many times I lost

The loves of my life have not been few
But I never could tell the false from the true
I thought each love would be mine till I'd die
But each love would die long before I

My only regret of all the loves that I knew
I never did find one that was honest and true
Somewhere on earth was a love meant for me
But I never was led to where it would be

But then again maybe one time love was there
But because of my youth I was not aware
The teachings of life are learned the first time around
For as hard as we try, second times are not found

I wonder, in death, is our life seen again
Can we go back in time, go back to when
We came to that fork, that fork in the road
And see if the other path offered a lighter load

WHAT IS A POET?

A poet is someone who lives in a dream
His world is make believe
He tries to live the beauty of life
But its birth he cannot conceive

A poet has feelings so deep in his soul
He sees all the beauty of living
He knows the true meaning of happiness lies
Not in the taking, but giving

He takes, not for granted, a newborn's cry
He cherishes drops of rain
He's sensitive to the wonders of life
And he feels, more than average, his pain

A poet sees not with only his eyes
To him the sky's not just air
The Moon, and the Stars, and the Sun in the sky
Are miracles, not "things" that are there

A poet may live his life all alone
Yet he knows he lives not in vain
For he gets his reward knowing people in love
Walk the sunshine he makes from rain

TO HAVE LOVED

AND

TO HAVE BEEN LOVED

IS TO HAVE NOT

LIVED IN VAIN

- Michael Colavito